Bible Promises
for Teens

Presented to _____

Given by _____

_____

_____

Date _____

For the Lord will give you
understanding in everything.
2 Timothy 2:7

Bible
Promises
for Teens

BROADMAN
& HOLMAN
PUBLISHERS

Nashville, Tennessee

Bible Promises for Teens
Copyright © 2003 by Broadman & Holman Publishers
All Rights Reserved

Broadman & Holman Publishers, Nashville, Tennessee
ISBN 10: 0-8054-2739-2
ISBN 13: 978-0-8054-2739-4

Dewey Decimal Classification: 242.5
Subject Heading: God–Promises/Promises/Teenagers

All Scripture verses are taken from the
HOLMAN CHRISTIAN STANDARD BIBLE®
Copyright © 1999, 2000, 2002, 2004
by Holman Bible Publishers

Printed in the United States
6 7 08 07 06

Contents

Promises for Everyday Decisions

Each day really does come with its share of decisions—some big, some small, some with very little riding on them, some with the potential to change the rest of your life.

But every decision you face does have one thing in common: the opportunity for you to either handle it your own way or to let God do the deciding for you and through you.

That's where the Bible comes in, because it covers so much ground and speaks to so many life issues. Let it speak to you today. Every day.

A Better Choice

What Makes God's Way the Best Way?

Whatever is true, whatever is honorable, whatever is just, whatever is pure, whatever is lovely, whatever is commendable—if there is any moral excellence and if there is any praise—dwell on these things.

Philippians 4:8

When all has been heard, the conclusion of the matter is this: fear God and obey His commandments, because this is all there is to being human.

Ecclesiastes 12:13

Therefore, whether you eat or drink, or whatever you do, do everything for God's glory.

1 Corinthians 10:31

You must follow the LORD your God and fear Him. You must keep His commands and listen to His voice; you must serve Him and remain faithful to Him.

Deuteronomy 13:4

You are not your own, for you were bought at a price; therefore glorify God in your body.

1 Corinthians 6:19-20

Take delight in the LORD, and He will give you your heart's desires.

Psalm 37:4

We could pretend that we're not in a war zone every day. But we'd be wrong. *The devil is constantly making sure that we have a hard time choosing right. So don't go into today without expecting a fight . . . and a way to win.*

No temptation has overtaken you except what is common to humanity. God is faithful and He will not allow you to be tempted beyond what you are able, but with the temptation He will also provide a way of escape, so that you are able to bear it.

1 Corinthians 10:13

Therefore, submit to God. But resist the Devil, and he will flee from you.

James 4:7

Don't give the Devil an opportunity.

Ephesians 4:27

He knows he has a short time.

Revelation 12:12

A Better Choice

Let us walk with decency, as in the daylight: not in carousing and drunkenness; not in sexual impurity and promiscuity; not in quarreling and jealousy. But put on the Lord Jesus Christ, and make no plans to satisfy the fleshly desires.

Romans 13:13-14

Don't throw away your confidence, which has a great reward. For you need endurance, so that after you have done God's will, you may receive what was promised.

Hebrews 10:35-36

Rejoice in hope; be patient in affliction; be persistent in prayer.

Romans 12:12

His divine power has given us everything required for life and godliness, through the knowledge of Him who called us by His own glory and goodness. By these He has given us very great and precious promises, so that through them you may share in the divine nature, escaping the corruption that is in the world because of evil desires.

For this very reason, make every effort to supplement your faith with goodness, goodness with knowledge, knowledge with self-control, self-control with endurance, endurance with godliness, godliness with brotherly affection, and brotherly affection with love. For if these qualities are yours and are increasing, they will keep you from being useless or unfruitful in the knowledge of our Lord Jesus Christ.

2 Peter 1:3-8

A Better Choice

Choices are made in the present, but the best ones have an eye on the future. *You have a whole lifetime ahead of you to reap the rewards of your decisions. What you do with today can make tomorrow a nice place to live.*

A noble person plans noble things; he stands up for noble causes.

Isaiah 32:8

So don't be foolish, but understand what the Lord's will is. And don't get drunk with wine, which leads to reckless actions, but be filled with the Spirit.

Ephesians 5:17-18

Don't be deceived: God is not mocked. For whatever a man sows he will also reap, because the one who sows to his flesh will reap corruption from the flesh, but the one who sows to the Spirit will reap eternal life from the Spirit.

Galatians 6:7-8

A Pleasing Sacrifice

Is There Anything I Wouldn't Do for You?

If anyone wants to be My follower, he must deny himself, take up his cross, and follow Me. For whoever wants to save his life will lose it, but whoever loses his life because of Me and the gospel will save it.

Mark 8:34-35

I have been crucified with Christ; and I no longer live, but Christ lives in me. The life I now live in the flesh, I live by faith in the Son of God, who loved me and gave Himself for me.

Galatians 2:19-20

So, you too consider yourselves dead to sin, but alive to God in Christ Jesus. Therefore do not let sin reign in your mortal body, so that you obey its desires. And do not offer any parts of it to sin as weapons for unrighteousness.

But as those who are alive from the dead, offer yourselves to God, and all the parts of yourselves to God as weapons for righteousness. For sin will not rule over you, because you are not under law but under grace.

Romans 6:11-14

Therefore, brothers, by the mercies of God, I urge you to present your bodies as a living sacrifice, holy and pleasing to God; this is your spiritual worship.

Romans 12:1

Christianity will cost you, but not as much as it pays you back in promises.
To live in the full experience of God's blessing, we have to part ways with the temporary tease of living for ourselves. We get eternity in exchange.

Do you not know that friendship with the world is hostility toward God? So whoever wants to be the world's friend becomes God's enemy.

James 4:4

Do not love the world or the things that belong to the world. If anyone loves the world, love for the Father is not in him. Because everything that belongs to the world—the lust of the flesh, the lust of the eyes, and the pride in one's lifestyle—is not from the Father, but is from the world. And the world with its lust is passing away, but the one who does God's will remains forever.

1 John 2:15-17

A Pleasing Sacrifice

If the world hates you, understand that it
hated Me before it hated you. If you were of
the world, the world would love you as its own.
However, because you are not of the world,
but I have chosen you out of the world, this
is why the world hates you.

John 15:18-19

I will look favorably on this kind of person:
one who is humble, submissive in spirit, and
trembles at My word.

Isaiah 66:2

Whoever does not bear his own cross and
come after Me cannot be My disciple.

Luke 14:27

Everything that was a gain to me, I have considered to be a loss because of Christ. More than that, I also consider everything to be a loss in view of the surpassing value of knowing Christ Jesus my Lord. Because of Him I have suffered the loss of all things and consider them filth, so that I may gain Christ and be found in Him, not having a righteousness of my own from the law, but one that is through faith in Christ—the righteousness from God based on faith.

My goal is to know Him and the power of His resurrection and the fellowship of His sufferings, being conformed to His death, assuming that I will somehow reach the resurrection from among the dead.

Philippians 3:7-11

Jesus knows how hard this life can be. So you can trust Him. He's been there. *There's no sacrifice you'll be asked to make as a believer that Christ hasn't already made Himself. He made it for you. And He'll be here to help.*

Therefore, since Christ suffered in the flesh, arm yourselves also with the same resolve— because the One who suffered in the flesh has finished with sin—in order to live the remaining time in the flesh, no longer for human desires, but for God's will.

1 Peter 4:1-2

For it was fitting, in bringing many sons to glory, that He, for whom and through whom all things exist, should make the source of their salvation perfect through sufferings.

Hebrews 2:10

I thought about my ways and turned my steps back to Your decrees. I hurried, not hesitating to keep Your commands.

Psalm 119:59-60

A Fresh Start

How Do I Get Up after I Goof Up?

Out of the depths I call to You, LORD! Lord, listen to my voice; let Your ears be attentive to my cry for help. LORD, if You considered sins, Lord, who could stand? But with You there is forgiveness, so that You may be revered.

Psalm 130:1-3

I said, "LORD, be gracious to me; heal me, for I have sinned against You."

Psalm 41:4

If we say, "We have no sin," we are deceiving ourselves, and the truth is not in us. If we confess our sins, He is faithful and righteous to forgive us our sins and to cleanse us from all unrighteousness.

1 John 1:8-9

And if My people who are called by My name humble themselves, pray and seek My face, and turn from their evil ways, then I will hear from heaven, forgive their sin, and heal their land.

2 Chronicles 7:14

You do not want a sacrifice, or I would give it; You are not pleased with a burnt offering. The sacrifice pleasing to God is a broken spirit. God, You will not despise a broken and humbled heart.

Psalm 51:16-17

We can get in some pretty deep water. But none that God can't pull us out of.
The troubles we find ourselves in can cause us a lot of heartache, pain, and regret. But they can't put us out of reach or beyond the hope of rescue.

He reached down from on high and took hold of me; He pulled me out of deep water.
Psalm 18:16

For troubles without number have surrounded me; my sins have overtaken me; I am unable to see. They are more than the hairs of my head, and my courage leaves me. LORD, be pleased to deliver me; hurry to help me, LORD.
Psalm 40:12-13

The salvation of the righteous is from the LORD, their refuge in a time of distress. The LORD helps and delivers them; He will deliver them from the wicked and will save them because they take refuge in Him.
Psalm 37:39-40

Now if the wicked turns away from all his sins that he has done, and keeps all My statutes and practices justice and righteousness, he will surely live; he will not die. None of the transgressions that he has done will be remembered against him; because of the righteousness which he has done he will live.

Do you actually think that I take pleasure in the death of the wicked, declares the Lord GOD, and not rather that he should turn away from his ways, and live?

Ezekiel 18:21-23

This is what the LORD says: If you return, I will restore you; you will stand in My presence.

Jeremiah 15:19

Wash away my guilt, and cleanse me from my sin. For I am conscious of my rebellion, and my sin is always before me.

Against You—You alone—I have sinned and done this evil in Your sight. . . .

Purify me with hyssop, and I will be clean; wash me, and I will be whiter than snow. Let me hear joy and gladness; let the bones You have crushed rejoice. Turn Your face away from my sins and blot out all my guilt.

God, create a clean heart for me and renew a steadfast spirit within me. Do not banish me from Your presence or take Your Holy Spirit from me. Restore the joy of Your salvation to me, and give me a willing spirit.

Psalm 51:2-4, 7-12

Feel like a failure sometimes? God can help put your best days ahead of you.
The shortest way out of guilt and despair is to own up to what you've done and throw yourself on God's mercy. You'll feel better soon—promise.

The LORD is compassionate and gracious, slow to anger and full of faithful love. He will not always accuse us or be angry forever. He has not dealt with us as our sins deserve or repaid us according to our offenses. For as high as the heavens are above the earth, so great is His faithful love toward those who fear Him. As far as the east is from the west, so far has He removed our transgressions from us.

Psalm 103:8-12

He brought me up from a desolate pit, out of the muddy clay, and set my feet on a rock, making my steps secure. He put a new song in my mouth, a hymn of praise to our God.

Psalm 40:2-3

A Real Freedom

What's the Feeling of Obedience?

Taste and see that the LORD is good. How happy is the man who takes refuge in Him! Fear the LORD, you His saints, for those who fear Him lack nothing. Young lions lack food and go hungry, but those who seek the LORD will not lack any good thing.

Psalm 34:8-10

Now the Lord is the Spirit; and where the Spirit of the Lord is, there is freedom. We all, with unveiled faces, are reflecting the glory of the Lord and are being transformed into the same image from glory to glory; this is from the Lord who is the Spirit.

2 Corinthians 3:17-18

He gave Himself for us to redeem us from all lawlessness and to cleanse for Himself a special people, eager to do good works.

Titus 2:14

How happy are those whose way is blameless, who live according to the law of the LORD! Happy are those who keep His decrees and seek Him with all their heart.

Psalm 119:1-2

Why do you spend money on what is not food, and your wages on what does not satisfy? Listen carefully to Me, and eat what is good, and you will enjoy the choicest of foods.

Isaiah 55:2

It's the difference between darkness and light, between trash and treasure. *There is just no comparison. The joy of living in close, uncluttered relationship with God gives you something you simply can't find anywhere else.*

The hope of the righteous is joy, but the expectation of the wicked comes to nothing.

Proverbs 10:28

The path of the righteous is like the light of dawn, shining brighter and brighter until midday. But the way of the wicked is like the darkest gloom; they don't know what makes them stumble.

Proverbs 4:18-19

Do not be conformed to this age, but be transformed by the renewing of your mind, so that you may discern what is the good, pleasing, and perfect will of God.

Romans 12:2

Jesus stood up and cried out, "If anyone is thirsty, he should come to Me and drink! The one who believes in Me, as the Scripture has said, will have streams of living water flow from deep within him."

John 7:37-38

The one who pursues righteousness and faithful love will find life, righteousness, and honor.

Proverbs 21:21

The humble will eat and be satisfied; those who seek the LORD will praise Him.

Psalm 22:26

How happy is the man who does not follow the advice of the wicked, or take the path of sinners, or join a group of mockers! Instead, his delight is in the LORD's instruction, and he meditates on it day and night.

He is like a tree planted beside streams of water that bears its fruit in season and whose leaf does not wither. Whatever he does prospers. The wicked are not like this; instead, they are like husks that the wind blows away.

Therefore the wicked will not survive the judgment, and sinners will not be in the community of the righteous. For the LORD watches over the way of the righteous, but the way of the wicked leads to ruin.

Psalm 1:1-6

Sin can sound like a whole lot of fun, but it comes back to bite you in the end. *There's no substitute for the rewards of obedience: peace of mind, a pure heart, the inner balance of knowing that you're the person you say you are.*

Now may the God of hope fill you with all joy and peace in believing, so that you may overflow with hope by the power of the Holy Spirit.

Romans 15:13

You reveal the path of life to me; in Your presence is abundant joy; in Your right hand are eternal pleasures.

Psalm 16:11

You have put more joy in my heart than they have when their grain and new wine abound. I will both lie down and sleep in peace, for You alone, LORD, make me live in safety.

Psalm 4:7-8

A Pure Difference

I Want to Live with a Clean Heart

I will live with integrity of heart in my house. I will not set anything godless before my eyes. I hate the doing of transgression; it will not cling to me. A devious heart will be far from me; I will not be involved with evil.

Psalm 101:2-4

Dear friends, if our hearts do not condemn us we have confidence before God, and can receive whatever we ask from Him because we keep His commands and do what is pleasing in His sight.

1 John 3:21-22

For this is what love for God is: to keep His commands. Now His commands are not a burden.

1 John 5:3

For we are His creation—created in Christ Jesus for good works, which God prepared ahead of time so that we should walk in them.

Ephesians 2:10

Therefore as you have received Christ Jesus the Lord, walk in Him, rooted and built up in Him and established in the faith, just as you were taught, and overflowing with thankfulness.

Colossians 2:6-7

Purity is a choice—a choice you make long before the alternative is offered.
You have been set apart by God to live a life that pleases Him, a life that will bless others and keep you protected. And it's a life worth doing right.

Now in a large house there are not only gold and silver bowls, but also those of wood and earthenware, some for special use, some for ordinary. So if anyone purifies himself from these things, he will be a special instrument, set apart, useful to the Master, prepared for every good work.

2 Timothy 2:20-21

For the one who wants to love life and to see good days must keep his tongue from evil and his lips from speaking deceit, and he must turn away from evil and do good. He must seek peace and pursue it, because the eyes of the Lord are on the righteous and His ears are open to their request.

1 Peter 3:10-12

Cleanse me from my hidden faults. Moreover, keep Your servant from willful sins; do not let them rule over me. Then I will be innocent, and cleansed from blatant rebellion. May the words of my mouth and the meditation of my heart be acceptable to You, O LORD, my rock and my Redeemer.

Psalm 19:12-14

You will keep in perfect peace the mind that is dependent on You, for it is trusting in You.

Isaiah 26:3

For me, living is Christ.

Philippians 1:21

For this is God's will, your sanctification: that you abstain from sexual immorality, so that each of you knows how to possess his own vessel in sanctification and honor, not with lustful desires, like the Gentiles who don't know God.

This means one must not transgress against and defraud his brother in this matter, because the Lord is an avenger of all these offenses, as we also previously told and warned you.

For God has not called us to impurity, but to sanctification. Therefore, the person who rejects this does not reject man, but God, who also gives you His Holy Spirit.

1 Thessalonians 4:3-8

The innocence of your character will communicate without saying a word.
Some people will give you a hard time about your high standards of living. But they're the ones who most need to see what faith looks like in real life.

Do everything without grumbling and arguing, so that you may be blameless and pure, children of God who are faultless in a crooked and perverted generation, among whom you shine like stars in the world.

Philippians 2:14-15

Commit your way to the LORD; trust in Him, and He will act, making your righteousness shine like the dawn, your justice like the noonday.

Psalm 37:5-6

Be alert, stand firm in the faith, be brave and strong. Your every action must be done with love.

1 Corinthians 16:13

Promises for Everyday Faith

You're not the first one to wonder whether all this Christianity stuff is really true. I mean, what if it's not? What if it's just a bunch of made-up ideas that you've inherited from your parents? And what gives it the right to say that it's the only way to God . . . with so many other ways to choose from?

Well, the Bible doesn't shrink away from dealing with questions like these. So let's open up and see what Christianity really means . . . and what it asks of those who take it seriously.

The Basics of Salvation

Remind Me Again What All This Means

God loved the world in this way: He gave His One and Only Son, so that everyone who believes in Him will not perish but have eternal life. For God did not send His Son into the world that He might judge the world, but that the world might be saved through Him.

John 3:16-17

Love consists in this: not that we loved God, but that He loved us and sent His Son.

1 John 4:10

This saying is trustworthy and deserving of full acceptance: "Christ Jesus came into the world to save sinners"—and I am the worst of them. But I received mercy because of this, so that in me, the worst of them, Christ Jesus might demonstrate the utmost patience.

1 Timothy 1:15-16

Whoever confesses that Jesus is the Son of God—God remains in him and he in God.

1 John 4:15

There is salvation in no one else, for there is no other name under heaven given to people by which we must be saved.

Acts 4:12

How will we escape if we neglect such a great salvation?

Hebrews 2:3

We wouldn't have required such love if it weren't for a big problem we had.
The moment we came into the world, we were already sinful and in need of a Savior. For us to approach a holy God, He had to change us first.

The LORD's hand is not too short to save, and His ear is not too deaf to hear. But your iniquities have built barriers between you and your God, and your sins have made Him hide His face from you so that He does not listen.

Isaiah 59:1-2

Your guilty acts have diverted these things from you. Your sins have withheld the bounty from you.

Jeremiah 5:25

But God, who is abundant in mercy, because of His great love that He had for us, made us alive with the Messiah even though we were dead in trespasses.

Ephesians 2:4-5

The Basics of Salvation

While we were still helpless, at the appointed moment, Christ died for the ungodly. For rarely will someone die for a just person—though for a good person perhaps someone might even dare to die. But God proves His own love for us in that while we were still sinners Christ died for us! . . . For if, while we were enemies, we were reconciled to God through the death of His Son, then how much more, having been reconciled, will we be saved by His life!

Romans 5:6-8, 10

Therefore, since we have been declared righteous by faith, we have peace with God through our Lord Jesus Christ.

Romans 5:1

This is the message of faith that we proclaim: if you confess with your mouth, "Jesus is Lord," and believe in your heart that God raised Him from the dead, you will be saved.

With the heart one believes, resulting in righteousness, and with the mouth one confesses, resulting in salvation.

Now the Scripture says, "No one who believes on Him will be put to shame," for there is no distinction between Jew and Greek, since the same Lord of all is rich to all who call on Him. For "everyone who calls on the name of the Lord will be saved."

Romans 10:8-13

The Basics of Salvation

In Him our sin has been dealt with, our soul reborn, our hope made secure.
God's free gift of salvation changes you into an entirely new creation—a person who no longer needs to fear the past, the present, or the future.

What then are we to say about these things? If God is for us, who is against us? He did not even spare His own Son, but offered Him up for us all; how will He not also with Him grant us everything?

Romans 8:31-32

For by grace you are saved through faith, and this is not from yourselves; it is God's gift— not from works, so that no one can boast.

Ephesians 2:8-9

But to all who did receive Him, He gave them the right to be children of God, to those who believe in His name, who were born, not of blood, or of the will of the flesh, or of the will of man, but of God.

John 1:12-13

The Demands of Discipline

What Should I Expect as a Christian?

Consider it a great joy, my brothers, whenever
you experience various trials, knowing that
the testing of your faith produces endurance.
But endurance must do its complete work,
so that you may be mature and complete,
lacking nothing.

James 1:2-4

We are not obligated to the flesh to live according to the flesh, for if you live according to the flesh, you are going to die. But if by the Spirit you put to death the deeds of the body, you will live.

Romans 8:12-13

Therefore, get your minds ready for action, being self-disciplined, and set your hope completely on the grace to be brought to you at the revelation of Jesus Christ.

As obedient children, do not be conformed to the desires of your former ignorance but, as the One who called you is holy, you also are to be holy in all your conduct; for it is written, "Be holy, because I am holy."

1 Peter 1:13-16

Each person should examine his own work, and then he will have a reason for boasting in himself alone, and not in respect to someone else. For each person will have to carry his own load.

Galatians 6:4-5

Living for God is the best thing going, but it still requires a lot of hard work.
The dots aren't always connected, the lines aren't always colored in, but those who commit their way to the Lord find the result worth the effort.

Without faith it is impossible to please God, for the one who draws near to Him must believe that He exists and rewards those who seek Him.

Hebrews 11:6

I will instruct you and show you the way to go; with My eye on you, I will give counsel. Do not be like a horse or mule, without understanding, that must be controlled with bit and bridle, or else it will not come near you.

Psalm 32:8-9

I love those who love me, and those who search for me find me.

Proverbs 8:17

Do you not know that the runners in a stadium all race, but only one receives the prize? Run in such a way that you may win. Now everyone who competes exercises self-control in everything. However, they do it to receive a perishable crown, but we an imperishable one. Therefore I do not run like one who runs aimlessly, or box like one who beats the air. Instead, I discipline my body and bring it under strict control, so that after preaching to others, I myself will not be disqualified.

1 Corinthians 9:24-27

Do not lack diligence; be fervent in spirit; serve the Lord.

Romans 12:11

What son is there whom a father does not discipline? But if you are without discipline—which all receive—then you are illegitimate children and not sons.

Furthermore, we had natural fathers discipline us, and we respected them. Shouldn't we submit even more to the Father of spirits and live? For they disciplined us for a short time based on what seemed good to them, but He does it for our benefit, so that we can share His holiness.

No discipline seems enjoyable at the time, but painful. Later on, however, it yields the fruit of peace and righteousness to those who have been trained by it.

Hebrews 12:7-11

Those who've been at this the longest will tell you: God is always faithful.
If you want to see the goodness of God in all its vivid colors, throw yourself into following Him with everything you've got. And then, you'll see.

Who then is a faithful and sensible slave, whom his master has put in charge of his household, to give him food at the proper time? Blessed is that slave whom his master, when he comes, will find working. I assure you: He will put him in charge of all his possessions.

Matthew 24:45-47

O God, You are my God; I eagerly seek You.

Psalm 63:1

With the faithful You prove Yourself faithful; with the blameless man You prove Yourself blameless; with the pure You prove Yourself pure.

Psalm 18:25-26

The Struggle of Doubt

Sometimes, I'm Not So Sure about This

What then? If some did not believe, will their unbelief cancel God's faithfulness? Absolutely not! God must be true, but everyone is a liar, as it is written: "That You may be justified in Your words and triumph when You judge."

Romans 3:3-4

Now faith is the reality of what is hoped for, the proof of what is not seen.

Hebrews 11:1

Faith comes from what is heard, and what is heard comes through the message about Christ.

Romans 10:17

Now if any of you lacks wisdom, he should ask God, who gives to all generously and without criticizing, and it will be given to him.

But let him ask in faith without doubting. For the doubter is like the surging sea, driven and tossed by the wind. That person should not expect to receive anything from the Lord. An indecisive man is unstable in all his ways.

James 1:5-8

And I pray this: that your love will keep on growing in knowledge and every kind of discernment, so that you can determine what really matters and can be pure and blameless in the day of Christ.

Philippians 1:9-10

You hear a lot of people saying a lot of different things. They can't all be right. *Just because something sounds good doesn't mean it can stand the test of time and experience. It's natural to doubt, but it's dangerous to stay there.*

Many deceivers have gone out into the world.
2 John 7

If anyone teaches other doctrine and does not agree with the sound teaching of our Lord Jesus Christ and with the teaching that promotes godliness, he is conceited, understanding nothing, but having a sick interest in disputes and arguments over words.

1 Timothy 6:3-4

For the time will come when they will not tolerate sound doctrine, but according to their own desires, will accumulate teachers for themselves because they have an itch to hear something new.

2 Timothy 4:3

But reject foolish and ignorant disputes, knowing that they breed quarrels. The Lord's slave must not quarrel, but must be gentle to everyone, able to teach, and patient, instructing his opponents with gentleness. Perhaps God will grant them repentance to know the truth. Then they may come to their senses and escape the Devil's trap, having been captured by him to do his will.

2 Timothy 2:23-26

My brothers, if any among you strays from the truth, and someone turns him back, he should know that whoever turns a sinner from the error of his way will save his life from death and cover a multitude of sins.

James 5:19-20

After eight days His disciples were indoors again, and Thomas was with them. Even though the doors were locked, Jesus came and stood among them. . . .

Then He said to Thomas, "Put your finger here and observe My hands. Reach out your hand and put it into My side. Don't be an unbeliever, but a believer."

Thomas responded to Him, "My Lord and my God!"

Jesus said, "Because you have seen Me, you have believed. Blessed are those who believe without seeing."

John 20:26-29

Ask God to make these things plain to you. He'll give you what you need. *Some matters will always remain in the mysteries of God. But answer this: Do you want a God so small, you can figure Him out in your own head?*

As for you, keep a clear head about everything.
2 Timothy 4:5

Then we will no longer be little children, tossed by the waves and blown around by every wind of teaching, by human cunning with cleverness in the techniques of deceit.
Ephesians 4:14

A man's steps are determined by the LORD, so how can anyone understand his own way?
Proverbs 20:24

But seek first the kingdom of God and His righteousness, and all these things will be provided for you.
Matthew 6:33

The Victory of Truth

God's Word Will Win Out in the End

As He was saying these things, many believed in Him. So Jesus said to the Jews who had believed Him, "If you continue in My word, you really are My disciples. You will know the truth, and the truth will set you free."

John 8:30-32

I know that all God accomplishes will last forever. Nothing can be added to it, and nothing can be taken away from it. God works so people may stand in awe of Him.

Ecclesiastes 3:14

Therefore, know that the LORD your God is God, the faithful God who keeps covenant loyalty to a thousandth generation for those who love Him and keep His commandments.

Deuteronomy 7:9

Let us draw near with a true heart in full assurance of faith, our hearts sprinkled clean from an evil conscience and our bodies washed in pure water. Let us hold on to the confession of our hope without wavering, for He who promised is faithful.

Hebrews 10:22-23

This God, our God forever and ever—He will lead us eternally.

Psalm 48:14

God's way has been proven true over the years. It will stay true to the end.
Try not to work so hard figuring and wondering whether or not His Word is true. Just jump in the middle of His will and ride it all the way home.

We are asking that you may be filled with the knowledge of His will in all wisdom and spiritual understanding.

Colossians 1:9

For I will give you such words and a wisdom that none of your adversaries will be able to resist or contradict.

Luke 21:15

Don't forget my teaching, but let your heart keep my commands; for they will bring you many days, a full life, and well-being. Never let loyalty and faithfulness leave you. Tie them around your neck; write them on the tablet of your heart.

Proverbs 3:1-3

The Victory of Truth

The entirety of Your word is truth, and all Your righteous judgments endure forever.

Psalm 119:160

Long ago You established the earth, and the heavens are the work of Your hands. They will perish, but You will endure; all of them will wear out like clothing.

You will change them like a garment, and they will pass away. But You are the same, and Your years will never end.

Psalm 102:25-27

Jesus Christ is the same yesterday, today, and forever.

Hebrews 13:8

Every spirit who confesses that Jesus Christ has come in the flesh is from God. But every spirit who does not confess Jesus is not from God. This is the spirit of the antichrist; you have heard that he is coming, and he is already in the world now.

You are from God, little children, and you have conquered them, because the One who is in you is greater than the one who is in the world. They are from the world. Therefore what they say is from the world, and the world listens to them.

We are from God. Anyone who knows God listens to us; anyone who is not from God does not listen to us. From this we know the Spirit of truth and the spirit of deception.

1 John 4:2-6

We're not afraid of anything, because we know that His truth will stand up.
Don't let anyone make you feel like you're not using your brain to believe in God. Everything comes together to say that God is who He says.

As for you, continue in what you have learned and firmly believed, knowing those from whom you learned, and that from childhood you have known the sacred Scriptures, which are able to instruct you for salvation through faith in Christ Jesus.

2 Timothy 3:14-15

Be diligent to present yourself approved to God, a worker who doesn't need to be ashamed, correctly teaching the word of truth.

2 Timothy 2:15

Then you will understand the fear of the LORD and discover the knowledge of God. For the LORD gives wisdom.

Proverbs 2:5-6

Promises for Everyday Worship

What can you do with your Christian faith? Is it something that sort of exists on its own, over there, on Sunday mornings or whenever it seems helpful to pull it out and put it on?

Or have you discovered yet that Christianity can come into play on Tuesdays at lunchtime, Thursdays after school, Saturday nights when fun and faith aren't accustomed to being seen out together?

Living with Christ is an everyday experience that adds much more to life than it takes away.

Losing Yourself in Praise

I Want to Be an All-Day Worshiper

Happy are the people who know the joyful shout; LORD, they walk in the light of Your presence. They rejoice in Your name all day long, and they are exalted by Your righteousness. For You are their magnificent strength.

Psalm 89:15-17

It is good to praise the LORD, to sing praise to Your name, Most High, to declare Your faithful love in the morning and Your faithfulness at night.

Psalm 92:1-2

My mouth will tell about Your righteousness and Your salvation all day long, though I cannot sum them up.

Psalm 71:15

Better a day in Your courts than a thousand anywhere else. I would rather be at the door of the house of my God than to live in the tents of the wicked.

Psalm 84:10

Therefore, through Him let us continually offer up to God a sacrifice of praise, that is, the fruit of our lips that confess His name.

Hebrews 13:15

My praise is always about You.

Psalm 71:6

When you think about all God has done for us, thanks is all you can say.
How do you respond to Jesus' sacrifice on the cross and the salvation He has given to you and all His people? You fall on your knees . . . and worship.

Come, let us worship and bow down; let us kneel before the LORD our Maker. For He is our God, and we are the people of His pasture, the sheep under His care.

Psalm 95:6-7

We all went astray like sheep; we all have turned to our own way. and the LORD has punished Him for the iniquity of all of us.

Isaiah 53:6

For you know the grace of our Lord Jesus Christ: although He was rich, for your sake He became poor, so that by His poverty you might become rich.

2 Corinthians 8:9

Oh, the depth of the riches both of the wisdom and the knowledge of God! How unsearchable His judgments and untraceable His ways! For who has known the mind of the Lord? Or who has been His counselor? Or who has ever first given to Him, and has to be repaid? For from Him and through Him and to Him are all things.

Romans 11:33-36

Sing to the LORD, for He has done glorious things. Let this be known throughout the earth.

Isaiah 12:5

From the rising of the sun to its setting, let the name of the LORD be praised.

Psalm 113:3

Shout triumphantly
  to the LORD, all the earth.
Serve the LORD with gladness;
  come before Him with joyful songs.
Acknowledge that the LORD is God.
  He made us, and we are His—
  His people, the sheep of His pasture.
Enter His gates with thanksgiving
  and His courts with praise.
Give thanks to Him
  and praise His name.
For the LORD is good,
  and His love is eternal;
His faithfulness endures
  through all generations.

Psalm 100:1-5

Now would be a good time to stop
what you're doing and praise the Lord.
*It doesn't have to be any special words—just the
awe and gratitude in your heart, coming out in
thoughts as numerous as you want to make them.*

Whom do I have in heaven but You? And I
desire nothing on earth but You. My flesh and
my heart may fail, but God is the strength of
my heart, my portion forever.

Psalm 73:25-26

You turned my lament into dancing; You
removed my sackcloth and clothed me with
gladness, so that I can sing to You and not be
silent. LORD my God, I will praise You forever.

Psalm 30:11-12

Let all who seek You rejoice and be glad in You;
let those who love Your salvation continually
say, "Great is the LORD!"

Psalm 40:16

Seeking God in Prayer

I Need to Know You're Always Near

When, on my bed, I think of You, I meditate on You during the night watches because You are my help; I will rejoice in the shadow of Your wings. I follow close to You; Your right hand holds on to me.

Psalm 63:6-8

I call to You for help, LORD; in the morning my prayer meets You.

Psalm 88:13

At daybreak, LORD, You hear my voice; at daybreak I plead my case to You and watch expectantly.

Psalm 5:3

Let me experience Your faithful love in the morning, for I trust in You. Reveal to me the way I should go, because I long for You. Rescue me from my enemies, LORD; I come to You for protection. Teach me to do Your will, for You are my God. May Your gracious Spirit lead me on level ground.

Psalm 143:8-10

Be gracious to me, LORD, for I call to You all day long. Bring joy to Your servant's life, since I set my hope on You, LORD. For You, LORD, are kind and ready to forgive, abundant in faithful love to all who call on You.

Psalm 86:3-5

**He is always there to hear your prayer.
So always be there to visit with Him.**
*Isn't it wonderful to know that there isn't a single
place you'll be today where God won't be as close
as your next thought, as near as your next breath?*

Don't worry about anything, but in everything, through prayer and petition with thanksgiving, let your requests be made known to God.
And the peace of God, which surpasses every
thought, will guard your hearts and your
minds in Christ Jesus.

Philippians 4:6-7

Now this is the confidence we have before
Him: whenever we ask anything according to
His will, He hears us. And if we know that He
hears whatever we ask, we know that we have
what we have asked Him for.

1 John 5:14-15

My God will hear me.

Micah 7:7

Therefore, since we have a great high priest who has passed through the heavens—Jesus the Son of God—let us hold fast to the confession. For we do not have a high priest who is unable to sympathize with our weaknesses, but One who has been tested in every way as we are, yet without sin. Therefore let us approach the throne of grace with boldness, so that we may receive mercy and find grace to help us at the proper time.

Hebrews 4:14-16

In the same way the Spirit also joins to help in our weakness. . . . He intercedes for the saints according to the will of God.

Romans 8:26-27

You should pray like this:
  Our Father in heaven,
    Your name be honored as holy.
  Your kingdom come.
    Your will be done
    on earth as it is in heaven.
  Give us today our daily bread.
    And forgive us our debts,
    as we also have forgiven our debtors.
  And do not bring us into temptation,
    but deliver us from the evil one.
  For Yours is the kingdom and the power
    and the glory forever. Amen.

Matthew 6:9-13

If you don't know what to say, just sit in the silence. Let Him do the talking. *God understands that prayer goes against our human nature. But learning to walk with Him everywhere we go leads to true spiritual victory.*

The LORD is near all who call out to Him, all who call out to Him with integrity. He fulfills the desires of those who fear Him; He hears their cry for help and saves them.

Psalm 145:18-19

Keep asking, and it will be given to you. Keep searching, and you will find. Keep knocking, and the door will be opened to you.

Matthew 7:7

Stay awake and pray, so that you won't enter into temptation. The spirit is willing, but the flesh is weak.

Matthew 26:41

Pray constantly.

1 Thessalonians 5:17

Finding Yourself in Stillness

Boy, Do I Need Some Quiet in My Life!

Come to Me, all you who are weary and burdened, and I will give you rest. Take My yoke upon you and learn from Me, because I am gentle and humble in heart, and you will find rest for your souls.

Matthew 11:28-29

Be silent before the LORD and wait expectantly for Him.

Psalm 37:7

Rest in God alone, my soul, for my hope comes from Him. He alone is my rock and my salvation, my stronghold; I will not be shaken. My salvation and glory depend on God; my strong rock, my refuge, is in God. Trust in Him at all times, you people; pour out your hearts before Him.

Psalm 62:5-8

Go into your private room, shut your door, and pray to your Father who is in secret. And your Father who sees in secret will reward you.

Matthew 6:6

I will praise the LORD who counsels me—even at night my conscience instructs me. I keep the LORD in mind always. Because He is at my right hand, I will not be defeated.

Psalm 16:7-8

Getting alone with God is one of the best ways to keep sin out of your day. *Time with Him will help you remember that no one cares for you like He does. Being with Him just makes you want to be with Him more.*

The LORD is good to those who hope in Him—to the one who seeks Him. It is good for one to wait silently for the LORD's salvation.

Lamentations 3:25-26

The result of righteousness will be peace; the effect of righteousness will be quiet confidence forever. Then My people will dwell in a peaceful place, and in safe and restful dwellings.

Isaiah 32:17-18

Let us then make every effort to enter that rest, so that no one will fall into the same pattern of disobedience.

Hebrews 4:11

The one who lives under the protection of the Most High dwells in the shadow of the Almighty.

Psalm 91:1

God, Your faithful love is so valuable that people take refuge in the shadow of Your wings. They are filled from the abundance of Your house; You let them drink from Your refreshing stream, for with You is life's fountain. In Your light we will see light.

Psalm 36:7-9

Calmness puts great sins to rest.

Ecclesiastes 10:4

The LORD is my shepherd; there is nothing I lack. He lets me lie down in green pastures; He leads me beside quiet waters. He renews my life; He leads me along the right paths for His name's sake.

Even when I go through the darkest valley, I am not afraid of any danger, for You are with me; Your rod and Your staff—they give me comfort.

You prepare a table before me in full view of my enemies; You anoint my head with oil; my cup is full.

Only goodness and faithful love will pursue me all the days of my life, and I will dwell in the house of the LORD as long as I live.

Psalm 23:1-6

We have so much to learn. I wonder if we can be still long enough to do it? *Life can get pretty noisy, pretty busy, pretty out of control at times. But those are actually the days when we most need to hear what He's saying.*

Call to Me and I will answer you and tell you great and mysterious things you do not know.

Jeremiah 33:3

The hidden things belong to the LORD our God, but the revealed things belong to us and our children forever, so that we may follow all the words of this law.

Deuteronomy 29:29

For nothing is concealed except to be revealed, and nothing hidden except to come to light.

Mark 4:22

Teach me, and I will be silent.

Job 6:24

Hearing God in the Bible

Help Me Understand What I'm Reading

Whatever was written before was written for our instruction, so that through our endurance and through the encouragement of the Scriptures we may have hope.

Romans 15:4

The LORD's works are great, studied by all who delight in them. All that He does is splendid and majestic; His righteousness endures forever.

Psalm 111:2-3

For the word of God is living and effective and sharper than any two-edged sword, penetrating as far as to divide soul, spirit, joints, and marrow; it is a judge of the ideas and thoughts of the heart.

Hebrews 4:12

Help me understand Your instruction, and I will obey it and follow it with all my heart.

Psalm 119:34

Open my eyes so that I may see wonderful things in Your law.

Psalm 119:18

Your promise has given me life.

Psalm 119:50

You never really understand the Bible until you start putting it into practice.
The Bible is a living book, the Christian's call to action. If you want to see it come to life for you, take it at face value . . . and live out its truth.

Be doers of the word and not hearers only, deceiving yourselves. Because if anyone is a hearer of the word and not a doer, he is like a man looking at his own face in a mirror; for he looks at himself, goes away, and right away forgets what kind of man he was. But the one who looks intently into the perfect law of freedom and perseveres in it, and is not a forgetful hearer but a doer who acts—this person will be blessed in what he does.

James 1:22-25

All Scripture is inspired by God . . . so that the man of God may be complete, equipped for every good work.

2 Timothy 3:17

Therefore, everyone who hears these words of Mine and acts on them will be like a sensible man who built his house on the rock. The rain fell, the rivers rose, and the winds blew and pounded that house. Yet it didn't collapse, because its foundation was on the rock.

But everyone who hears these words of Mine and doesn't act on them will be like a foolish man who built his house on the sand. The rain fell, the rivers rose, the winds blew and pounded that house, and it collapsed. And its collapse was great!

Matthew 7:24-27

I will not forget Your word.

Psalm 119:16

The instruction of the LORD
  is perfect, reviving the soul;
the testimony of the LORD is trustworthy,
  making the inexperienced wise.
The precepts of the LORD
  are right, making the heart glad;
the commandment of the LORD
  is radiant, making the eyes light up.
The fear of the LORD
  is pure, enduring forever;
the ordinances of the LORD
  are reliable and altogether righteous.
They are more desirable than gold—
  than an abundance of pure gold;
and sweeter than honey—
  than honey dripping from the comb.

Psalm 19:7-10

Make the Bible your treasure, and you'll be the richest person on earth.
You'll find yourself coming across new things in there all the time—your whole life long—for the Bible never gets old. It just keeps getting better.

Your word is a lamp for my feet and a light on my path.

Psalm 119:105

Your instruction resides within me.

Psalm 40:8

I rejoice in the way revealed by Your decrees as much as in all riches.

Psalm 119:14

I have treasured Your word in my heart so that I may not sin against You.

Psalm 119:11

I am resolved to obey Your statutes to the very end.

Psalm 119:112

Expressing Yourself in Words

Help Me Remember and Never Forget

I told You about my life, and You listened to me; teach me Your statutes. Help me understand the meaning of Your precepts so that I can meditate on Your wonders.

Psalm 119:26-27

My heart is moved by a noble theme as I recite my verses to the king; my tongue is the pen of a skillful writer.

Psalm 45:1

O that my words were written down! O that they were recorded on a scroll, or that with an iron stylus and lead they were inscribed in stone forever!

Job 19:23-24

Go, now write it on a tablet in their presence and inscribe it on a scroll; it will be for the future, forever and ever.

Isaiah 30:8

Therefore I will always remind you about these things, even though you know them and are established in the truth you have. I consider it right . . . to wake you up with a reminder.

2 Peter 1:12-13

Remember therefore what you have received and heard.

Revelation 3:3

Keeping a journal has a longstanding place in the history of God's people.
It wasn't uncommon at all for God to direct people to write down what He was doing, had done, or was about to do. See for yourself . . .

At the LORD's command, Moses wrote down the starting points for the stages of their journey.
Numbers 33:2

The word of the LORD came to me in the ninth year, in the tenth month, on the tenth day of the month: "Son of man, write down the name of this day, this very day."
Ezekiel 24:1-2

I, John, your brother and partner in the tribulation, kingdom, and perseverance in Jesus, was on the island called Patmos because of God's word and the testimony about Jesus. I was in the Spirit on the Lord's day, and I heard behind me a loud voice like a trumpet saying, "Write on a scroll what you see."
Revelation 1:9-11

Just reflecting on my affliction and homelessness brings gall and poison. You must certainly recall that my soul has been brought low within me.

This I bring to mind; therefore, I will have hope. The LORD's faithful love does not cease, His compassions have no end. They are new every morning; great is Your faithfulness. "The LORD is my only inheritance," says my soul; therefore, I will place my hope in Him.

Lamentations 3:19-24

Remember your Creator in the days of your youth: while the evil days are still in the future, and the years have not arrived that will cause you to say, "I have no delight in them."

Ecclesiastes 12:1

These words that I am giving you today are to be in your heart. . . . Bind them as a sign on your hand and let them be a symbol on your forehead. Write them on the doorposts of your house and on your gates.

When the LORD your God brings you into the land . . . with large and beautiful cities that you did not build, houses full of every good thing that you did not fill them with, wells dug that you did not dig, and vineyards and olive groves that you did not plant—and when you eat and are satisfied, be careful not to forget the LORD who brought you out of the land of Egypt, out of the place of slavery.

Deuteronomy 6:6, 8-12

Tracking your journey with God will give you a visible record of confidence. *When you look back from down the road, and reflect on how He led you through a really tough time, you'll remember that He can do it again.*

Remember the earlier days when, after you had been enlightened, you endured a hard struggle with sufferings.

Hebrews 10:32

You Yourself have recorded my wanderings. Put my tears in Your bottle. Are they not in Your records?

Psalm 56:8

See! Even now my Witness is in the heavens; my Advocate is in the heights. My Intercessor is my friend as my eyes drip with tears before God. He argues a man's case with God as a man would for his friend.

Job 16:19-21

Promises for Today, Forever

The Bible is a book that never gets tired or tiring—not to those who come to it each day with their hearts thirsty for a drink from God's refreshing fountain, hungry for a taste of living bread, aching from the tug and tension of teenage life and wondering how to make sense of the things rattling around in their heads.

Whether it's stuff happening at home or with your friends—or just yourself, your needs, and your future, the Bible gives you a place to turn that will always have something good to say.

At Home with Your Parents

I Really Cherish This Relationship

Children, obey your parents in the Lord, because this is right. Honor your father and mother—which is the first commandment with a promise—that it may go well with you and that you may have a long life in the land.

Ephesians 6:1-3

Listen, my son, to your father's instruction, and don't reject your mother's teaching, for they will be a garland of grace on your head and a gold chain around your neck.

Proverbs 1:8-9

Pay attention to my words; listen closely to my sayings. Don't lose sight of them.

Proverbs 4:20-21

Always bind them to your heart; tie them around your neck. When you walk here and there, they will guide you; when you lie down, they will watch over you; when you wake up, they will talk to you. For a commandment is a lamp, teaching is a light, and corrective instructions are the way to life.

Proverbs 6:20-23

Protect my teachings as you would the pupil of your eye. Tie them to your fingers; write them on the tablet of your heart.

Proverbs 7:2-3

Be careful that the words don't fly too freely at your house. They can hurt.

There's a sense of God's blessing that settles down in a home where everyone is committed to getting along, working together, and loving each other.

No man can tame the tongue. It is a restless evil, full of deadly poison. With it we bless our Lord and Father, and with it we curse men who are made in God's likeness. Out of the same mouth come blessing and cursing. My brothers, these things should not be this way.

James 3:8-10

Who is wise and understanding among you? He should show his works by good conduct with wisdom's gentleness. . . . The wisdom from above is first pure, then peace-loving, gentle, compliant, full of mercy and good fruits, without favoritism and hypocrisy. And the fruit of righteousness is sown in peace by those who make peace.

James 3:13, 17-18

Do not despise the LORD's instruction, my son, and do not loathe His discipline; for the Lord disciplines the one He loves, just as a father, the son he delights in.

Proverbs 3:11-12

The LORD's curse is on the household of the wicked, but He blesses the home of the righteous; He mocks those who mock, but gives grace to the humble. The wise will inherit honor, but He holds up fools to dishonor.

Proverbs 3:33-35

Each of you is to respect his mother and father.

Leviticus 19:3

When I was a son with my father, tender and precious to my mother, he taught me and said: "Your heart must hold on to my words. Keep my commands and live. Get wisdom, get understanding; don't forget or turn away from the words of my mouth. Don't abandon wisdom, and she will watch over you; love her, and she will guard you. Wisdom is supreme— so get wisdom. And whatever else you get, get understanding. Cherish her, and she will exalt you; if you embrace her, she will honor you. She will place a garland of grace on your head; she will give you a crown of beauty."

Proverbs 4:3-9

Your love, respect, and prayers mean more to your parents than anything. *Sure, your parents are your authority. Yet the experience of joining them in making a home is one of the most wonderful things you can do.*

I urge that petitions, prayers, intercessions, and thanksgivings be made for everyone . . . in authority, so that we may lead a tranquil and quiet life in all godliness and dignity.

1 Timothy 2:1-2

There is no authority except from God, and those that exist are instituted by God. So then, the one who resists the authority is opposing God's command.

Romans 13:1-2

Obey your leaders and submit to them, for they keep watch over your souls as those who will give an account, so that they can do this with joy and not with grief, for that would be unprofitable for you.

Hebrews 13:17

In Tune with Your Friends

I Owe These Guys a Lot

Now may the God of endurance and encouragement grant you agreement with one another, according to Christ Jesus, so that you may glorify the God and Father of our Lord Jesus Christ with a united mind and voice.

Romans 15:5-6

Each one of us must please his neighbor for his good, in order to build him up.

Romans 15:2

For none of us lives to himself, and no one dies to himself. If we live, we live to the Lord.

Romans 14:7-8

As we have many parts in one body, and all the parts do not have the same function, in the same way we who are many are one body in Christ and individually members of one another.

Romans 12:4-5

Two are better than one because they receive good payment for their struggles. For if one of them falls, his companion can help him up. But woe to the one who falls alone with no one to help him up. . . . Though an assailant might overpower one, two can resist him. A rope with three strands does not quickly snap.

Ecclesiastes 4:9-10, 12

Not everyone makes a good friend.
We tend to become who we're around.

God calls us to love everybody. But when it comes to the matter of ongoing friendship, the Bible is just as clear that we should be careful, cautious.

Don't make friends with an angry man, and don't be a companion of a hot-tempered man, or you will learn his ways and entangle yourself in a snare.

Proverbs 22:24-25

The one who walks with the wise will become wise, but a companion of fools will suffer harm.

Proverbs 13:20

Do not be deceived: "Bad company corrupts good morals."

1 Corinthians 15:33

For the assembly of the godless will be fruitless.

Job 15:34

I am a friend to all who fear You, to those who keep Your precepts.

Psalm 119:63

A man with many friends may be harmed, but there is a friend who stays closer than a brother.

Proverbs 18:24

Iron sharpens iron, and one man sharpens another.

Proverbs 27:17

A friend loves at all times, and a brother is born for a difficult time.

Proverbs 17:17

Therefore, God's chosen ones, holy and loved, put on heartfelt compassion, kindness, humility, gentleness, and patience, accepting one another and forgiving one another if anyone has a complaint against another. Just as the Lord has forgiven you, so also you must forgive.

Above all, put on love—the perfect bond of unity. And let the peace of the Messiah, to which you were also called in one body, control your hearts. Be thankful.

Let the message about the Messiah dwell richly among you, teaching and admonishing one another in all wisdom, and singing psalms, hymns, and spiritual songs, with gratitude in your hearts to God.

Colossians 3:12-16

We owe our friends the gift of a godly example, the picture of a living witness. *We are created with both a desire and a need for friendship. But we are called to do more than soak up this blessing. We are called to give back to it.*

You are the light of the world. A city situated on a hill cannot be hidden. No one lights a lamp and puts it under a basket, but rather on a lampstand, and it gives light for all who are in the house. In the same way, let your light shine before men, so that they may see your good works and give glory to your Father in heaven.

Matthew 5:14-16

Set an example of good works yourself, with integrity and dignity.

Titus 2:7

Practice these things; be committed to them, so that your progress may be evident to all.

1 Timothy 4:15

At Peace with Yourself

Keep Me Growing, Maturing

I know both how to have a little, and I know how to have a lot. In any and all circumstances I have learned the secret of being content— whether well-fed or hungry, whether in abundance or in need. I am able to do all things through Him who strengthens me.

Philippians 4:12-13

Now everyone who lives on milk is inexperienced with the message about righteousness, because he is an infant. But solid food is for the mature—for those whose senses have been trained to distinguish between good and evil.

Hebrews 5:13-14

For when we were in the flesh, the sinful passions operated through the law in every part of us and bore fruit for death. But now we have been released from the law, since we have died to what held us, so that we may serve in the new way of the Spirit and not in the old letter of the law.

Romans 7:5-6

Based on the gift they have received, everyone should use it to serve others, as good managers of the varied grace of God. If anyone speaks, his speech should be like the oracles of God; if anyone serves, his service should be from the strength God provides, so that in everything God may be glorified through Jesus Christ.

1 Peter 4:10-11

Christianity is not an excuse for doing nothing. It's a reason to move, to grow. *Some people do little more with their faith than keep their church pew warm. But true followers of Christ are committed to burning up the road.*

I know nothing is better for anyone than to rejoice and to accomplish good with their lives.

Ecclesiastes 3:12

Now we want each of you to demonstrate the same diligence for the final realization of your hope, so that you won't become lazy, but imitators of those who inherit the promises through faith and perseverance.

Hebrews 6:11-12

Therefore, dear friends, since you have been forewarned, be on your guard, so that you are not led away by the error of the immoral and fall from your own stability. But grow in the grace and knowledge of our Lord and Savior Jesus Christ.

2 Peter 3:17-18

Watch out, brothers, so that there won't be in any of you an evil, unbelieving heart that departs from the living God. But encourage each other daily, while it is still called today, so that none of you is hardened by sin's deception. For we have become companions of the Messiah if we hold firmly until the end the reality that we had at the start.

Hebrews 3:12-14

Love must be without hypocrisy. Detest evil; cling to what is good.

Romans 12:9

And whatever you do, in word or in deed, do everything in the name of the Lord Jesus.

Colossians 3:17

Just as a branch is unable to produce fruit by itself unless it remains on the vine, so neither can you unless you remain in Me.

I am the vine; you are the branches. The one who remains in Me and I in him produces much fruit, because you can do nothing without Me. If anyone does not remain in Me, he is thrown aside like a branch and he withers. They gather them, throw them into the fire, and they are burned.

If you remain in Me and My words remain in you, ask whatever you want and it will be done for you. My Father is glorified by this: that you produce much fruit and prove to be My disciples.

John 15:4-8

Living for Jesus doesn't require as much "doing" as it does "depending." *Yes, there are lot of things to do in serving God. But in reality, it's more about learning to lean on Him, letting Him do all the work through you.*

We are asking that you may be filled with the knowledge of His will in all wisdom and spiritual understanding, so that you may walk worthy of the Lord, fully pleasing to Him, bearing fruit in every good work and growing in the knowledge of God.

Colossians 1:11

Be in agreement with one another. Do not be proud; instead, associate with the humble. Do not be wise in your own estimation. Do not repay anyone evil for evil. Try to do what is honorable in everyone's eyes. If possible, on your part, live at peace with everyone.

Romans 12:16-18

In Search of a Plan

How Can I Know God's Will for Me?

I know the plans I have for you," this is the solemn declaration of the LORD, "plans for well-being, not for disaster, to give you a future and hope. You will call to Me and come and pray to Me, and I will listen to you. You will seek Me and find Me when you search for Me with all your heart."

Jeremiah 29:11-13

We know that all things work together for the good of those who love God: those who are called according to His purpose.

Romans 8:28

The counsel of the LORD stands forever, the plans of His heart from generation to generation.

Psalm 33:11

Therefore don't worry about tomorrow, because tomorrow will worry about itself. Each day has enough trouble of its own.

Matthew 6:34

We have this kind of confidence toward God through Christ: not that we are competent in ourselves to consider anything as coming from ourselves, but our competence is from God.

2 Corinthians 3:4-5

May He give you what your heart desires and fulfill your whole purpose.

Psalm 20:4

The best way to plan for your future is to do what's in front of you today. *God rarely shows us where we'll be years from now, but if we'll watch for Him in our daily lives, we'll find ourselves doing His will all along.*

Don't worry about your life, what you will eat or what you will drink; or about your body, what you will wear. Isn't life more than food and the body more than clothing? Look at the birds of the sky: they don't sow or reap or gather into barns, yet your heavenly Father feeds them.

Matthew 6:25-26

For God has not given us a spirit of fearfulness, but one of power, love, and sound judgment.

2 Timothy 1:7

The plans of the diligent certainly lead to profit.

Proverbs 21:5

Not that I have already reached the goal
or am already fully mature, but I make every
effort to take hold of it because I also have
been taken hold of by Christ Jesus. Brothers,
I do not consider myself to have taken hold of
it. But one thing I do: forgetting what is behind
and reaching forward to what is ahead, I pursue as my goal the prize promised by God's
heavenly call in Christ Jesus.

Philippians 3:12-14

I know You can do anything; no plan of Yours
can be denied.

Job 42:2

Return to your rest, my soul,
for the LORD has been good to you.

Psalm 116:7

Promises for Today, Forever

I raise my eyes toward the mountains.
  Where will my help come from?
My help comes from the LORD,
  the Maker of heaven and earth.
He will not allow your foot to slip;
  your Protector will not slumber.
Indeed, the Protector of Israel
  does not slumber or sleep.
The LORD protects you;
  the LORD is a shelter right by your side.
The sun will not strike you by day,
  or the moon by night.
The LORD will protect you from all harm;
  He will protect your life.
The LORD will protect your coming and going
  both now and forever.

Psalm 121:1-8

In Search of a Plan

You can trust God to be faithful to lead you where He wants you to go.
The worst thing you can do in seeking God's will is to waste time worrying about it. It's His job to lead you there. It's your job just to follow.

Plans fail when there is no counsel, but with many advisers they succeed.

Proverbs 15:22

Commit your activities to the LORD and your plans will be achieved.

Proverbs 16:3

The LORD makes poor and gives wealth; He humbles and He exalts. He raises the poor from the dust and lifts the needy from the ash heap. He seats them with noblemen and grants them a throne of honor. For the foundations of the earth belong to the LORD; He has set the world on them. He guards the feet of His devout followers . . . for it is not through strength that a man prevails.

1 Samuel 2:7-9

At Last
in Eternity

Keep My Eyes on the Prize

Dear friends, we are God's children now, and
what we will be has not yet been revealed. We
know that when He appears, we will be like
Him, because we will see Him as He is. And
everyone who has this hope in Him purifies
himself just as He is pure.

1 John 3:2-3

Dear friends, don't let this one thing escape you: with the Lord one day is like 1,000 years, and 1,000 years like one day. The Lord does not delay His promise, as some understand delay, but is patient with you, not wanting any to perish, but all to come to repentance.

2 Peter 3:8-9

For God did not appoint us to wrath, but to obtain salvation through our Lord Jesus Christ, who died for us, so that whether we are awake or asleep, we will live together with Him.

1 Thessalonians 5:9-10

Therefore, brothers, be patient until the Lord's coming. See how the farmer waits for the precious fruit of the earth and is patient with it until he receives the early and the late rains. You also must be patient. Strengthen your hearts, because the Lord's coming is near.

James 5:7-8

This hope does not disappoint.

Romans 5:5

If receiving Christ feels good, wait till you receive all He's got coming to you.
Yes, being a Christian is the greatest thing in the world. And when this world is no more, living with Jesus will only become better than ever.

So if you have been raised with the Messiah, seek what is above, where the Messiah is, seated at the right hand of God. Set your minds on what is above, not on what is on the earth. . . . When the Messiah, who is your life, is revealed, then you also will be revealed with Him in glory.

Colossians 3:1-2, 4

For the grace of God has appeared, with salvation for all people, instructing us to deny godlessness and worldly lusts and to live in a sensible, righteous, and godly way in the present age, while we wait for the blessed hope and the appearing of the glory of our great God and Savior, Jesus Christ.

Titus 2:11-13

Therefore since we also have such a large
cloud of witnesses surrounding us, let us lay
aside every weight and the sin that so easily
ensnares us, and run with endurance the race
that lies before us, keeping our eyes on Jesus,
the source and perfecter of our faith, who for
the joy that lay before Him endured a cross
and despised the shame, and has sat down
at the right hand of God's throne.

Hebrews 12:1-2

He will transform the body of our humble
condition into the likeness of His glorious
body, by the power that enables Him to
subject everything to Himself.

Philippians 3:21

Then he showed me the river of living water, sparkling like crystal, flowing from the throne of God and of the Lamb down the middle of the broad street of the city.

On both sides of the river was the tree of life bearing 12 kinds of fruit, producing its fruit every month. The leaves of the tree are for healing the nations, and there will no longer be any curse.

The throne of God and of the Lamb will be in the city, and His servants will serve Him. They will see His face, and His name will be on their foreheads. Night will no longer exist, and people will not need lamplight or sunlight, because the Lord God will give them light. And they will reign forever and ever.

Revelation 22:1-5

Learn how to live with eternity in your eyes. It changes the look of everything. *One lifetime is just not long enough to experience the wonders of who God is and what He's done. Prepare to be loving Him for this . . . forever.*

He has given us a new birth into a living hope through the resurrection of Jesus Christ from the dead, and into an inheritance that is imperishable, uncorrupted, and unfading, kept in heaven for you, who are being protected by God's power through faith for a salvation that is ready to be revealed in the last time.

1 Peter 1:3-5

Therefore we do not give up; even though our outer person is being destroyed, our inner person is being renewed day by day.

2 Corinthians 4:16

I am sure of this, that He who started a good work in you will carry it on to completion until the day of Christ Jesus.

Philippians 1:6

*Look for these other Bible Promise books
to give to the special people in your life.*

**Bible Promises
for Mom**
0-8054-2732-5

**Bible Promises
for Dad**
0-8054-2733-3

**Bible Promises
for My Teacher**
0-8054-2734-1

**Bible Promises
for the Graduate**
0-8054-2741-4

**Bible Promises
for New Believers**
0-8054-2742-2

**Bible Promises
for New Parents**
0-8054-2738-4

 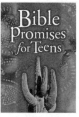

**Bible Promises
for Kids**
0-8054-2740-6

**Bible Promises
for Teens**
0-8054-2739-2